The Ground for Christian Ethics

T. M. Moore

1 Tim 6:13-16

Waxed Tablet
Publications

The Ground for Christian Ethics

1.   The Proposition

Instructor: Good morning, my friend. Ooh, why so glum?

Disciple: Glum is not the word. Disappointment mixed with confusion, festering into anger: that's what you're reading on my face.

I: And deep, I'd say. What has happened?

D: Nothing so unusual – at least, not any more. A friend of mine, a pastor, has resigned his ministry, left his wife and family, and refuses any contact with his friends. No one knows why, or if there's another woman, or what. He just up and left.

I: I'm so sorry. We must pray for that family and church, and for your friend. You're right – this situation is becoming increasingly familiar. It makes you wonder, doesn't it?

D: Makes me mad! Wonder about what?

I: Well, don't you wonder how a man who has made a Christian profession, has studied for and been ordained to the Gospel ministry, and has taught, counseled, and discipled others in the Christian faith, how such a man can have failed to embrace a Christian *ethic* for his own personal behavior?

D: I'm not past being mad yet, so I haven't begun thinking rationally about it. What makes you think he hasn't embraced a Christian ethic? I mean, I know he's done a foolish thing – at least, that's how it appears. He's not acting like a Christian should; that is, he's clearly in violation of a Christian ethic – although he may not think so – but does this mean he hasn't embraced a Christian ethic?

I: I agree with you: it appears that he has not *applied the principles* of a Christian ethic in this situation. Apparently he has made a decision affecting his marriage, family, ministry, church, and friends on what appear to be merely selfish grounds. Unless some unknown medical problem is to blame, I can see no other explanation for this decision other than, when push comes to shove, your friend prefers his own convenience and satisfaction to the needs and interests of others. Such a decision certainly does not represent the ethics of Christ and His Apostles. If your friend had embraced a Christian ethic as his own, surely he would have been able to summon the spiritual and moral resources to resist this unhappy course.

D: OK…

I: So I can only wonder why your friend, a student of the Bible and a minister of the Gospel, failed to embrace a Christian ethic, one sufficient to guide him in the good and loving way, no matter what. While doubtless he *affirmed* and even *taught* many of the principles of Christian and Biblical ethics, while he may even have *affirmed* and *professed* a Christian ethic, his *own* ethical conduct indicates that, at the most foundational level, he is thinking about himself more than his God or his neighbor. He has embraced some other ethic than that one that counsels us to resist the devil, hate evil, do unto others as we would have them do unto us, and lay down our lives for our friends. I wonder how that could be?

And further, I wonder what other stimuli he has subjected himself to over the years which led him to embrace an ethic of self-serving over one of laying down his life for others. For clearly, ethical *principles* have dictated his actions. He was acting on *some* ethical ground, weighing his choices and choosing a course of action within a framework of presuppositions, principles, and practices, the combination of which led to this most unhappy and disturbing course of action. Well, I wonder what *inputs* marked out the ground of his ethics and led to this sad situation? And what inputs, by contrast, should fertilize the ground of a *Christian* and *Biblical* ethic?

D: Your question troubles me, for it implies that merely *professing* Christ and *publicly identifying oneself* as His follower – even *serving* Him in the ministry – do not constitute a sufficient foundation for ensuring that one will *live* like Jesus in the ethics of everyday life.

I: That is indeed what I contend. And if this is the state of our *shepherds* – an increasingly familiar situation, as you noted – what does it imply concerning the state of their *flocks?*[1]

And may I risk troubling you even further? How would you respond to the suggestion that failure to *live* like Jesus in the daily ethical situations of life may well – I say, *may* – indicate that one's *profession* of Christ is unproven, and whatever *service* may have been rendered in His Name may actually be in vain? That is, might it be the case that failure to embrace the *ethics* of Jesus calls into question the validity of *any* claims of having *any* real, saving relationship with Him?[2]

D: I can't deny your suggestion, even though the idea of it disturbs me. This is perhaps the most troubling part of this situation. I've known this man for many years, and have admired his teaching and ministry. We have often talked together about the Lord, and I have seen much in his life that seems to support his testimony of faith. But I'm deeply disturbed by his flagrant act of selfishness, which, I hesitate to confess, causes me to question whether he truly knows the Lord.

I: Understandable. Yet we must be careful about presuming in this matter. Concerning this much, however, I think we may legitimately inquire: If merely professing Christ and being somehow publicly identified as a follower of the Lord, are not sufficient to engender a Christian ethic, then of what eternal value are such professions and acts of identification? For clearly, implied in Jesus' command that we should follow Him are the ideas that we should begin to adopt the same priorities, walk the same path, seek the same ends, and live the same ethic as He did.[3] But if our profession and act of public identification are not a sufficient *ground* for such an ethic, that ethic being the expected outworking of our confession, then something else, some other *ground*, must be sought out as the soil of which that ethic can come to fruition. Not, mind you, for *entering* into relationship with Christ, but for *validating* and *bringing to expression* the reality of that relationship, entered into by grace through faith.[4] And if that *ground*, whatever it may be, is alone sufficient to engender a truly Christian *ethic*, then can there be any true

---

[1] Luke 6.40
[2] Matthew 7.15-20
[3] 1 John 2.1-6
[4] Ephesians 2.8-10

3

relationship with Jesus where that *ground* is not fervently sought and diligently established, leading to the practice of that *ethic* to which Jesus Himself adhered? Where, in other words, must a true Christian take his stand in order to prepare himself, soul and body, to follow the way of the Lord, no matter the temptation or trial? Is there a *touchstone* for Christian ethics, a fount, a wellspring, recourse to which is incumbent upon all Christians, to which we may apply for wisdom and guidance in ethical decision-making? In short, what is the *ground* from which we may expect a true Christian profession to give rise to a flourishing Christian ethic?

D: I'm not sure I understand the way you are using the word, "ground."

I: I mean a kind of a launch-pad for ethical living, a starting-point from which one makes choices and decisions in ethical conduct – better, the soil within which the lovely flower of Christian ethical life may spring and bloom.

You see, every ethical system is established on some fundamental ground. Rationalism, for example, takes as its ground the functioning of reason – the laws of logic applied to questions of ethical conduct. Rationalism says that, if we can *reason* our way to a decision, in which inconsistencies, contradictions, *non sequitirs*, and the like are minimized or eliminated, then we shall have cause to believe that our decision is sound. The *ground* of a rationalistic ethic is *reason* and the laws of logic.

Existential ethical practices come to bloom from an altogether different ground. In an existential ethic reason and logic may, or may not, play a decisive role in what any individual chooses to do in any situation. Feeling and affections may be just as important, or intuition, or even mere whim. What matters in existential ethics is that each choice be *authentic*, one made solely by the choosing individual, drawing upon the resources of the moment, from within his own chest, as it were, and without regard to external pressures. The *ground* of existential ethics is therefore *self-authentication*, however that may be defined.

Similarly, a postmodern ethic takes root in a ground of *group-authentication*. One makes his or her ethical decisions as a member of a group, or community, and with reference to how the group would reinforce, approve, or help to facilitate those ethical choices. One may change his group, or even participate in many different groups at the same time, thus requiring him to learn the ethical protocols of each; what matters, however, is that loyalty to group identity be preserved and advanced. Such an ethic is plainly pragmatic and relativistic, yet it defines the ethical conduct of increasing numbers of people. The *ground* of a postmodern ethic is *group-authentication*.

D: So there is a similar "ground" for a Christian and Biblical ethic, one that goes beyond merely professing Jesus as Savior and Lord, and being identified with Him in some public way, such as church membership…

I: Or involvement in pastoral ministry.

D: …and that ground, fertile and well-tended, produces the fruit of Christian ethics over time. Where shall we look to discover this ground, where, as you say, the flower of true Christian ethics may bloom?

I: I think I could persuade you, if you are sufficiently open to the mind of Christ, to embrace the proposition that the only proper ground for a Christian and Biblical ethic is the Law of God.

D: Do I need persuading that this is so?

I: I'm not sure; however, if your experience of the Christian faith is like that of a great many others who name Him as Savior and Lord – like your pastor friend – I rather suspect that your present view of the Law of God is not yet at the level at which it truly and patently serves as the ground of your Christian ethic.

Shall we try a little test?

D: All right.

I: Fine. In your mind, can you name the Ten Commandments in order?

D: Give me a moment…I can name them, but I'm not sure they're in order. I mean, I'm sure they're *not* in order.

I: And you are a student of Scripture, one who is preparing for the Gospel ministry?

D: Yes, of course.
I: And yet you cannot name the Ten Commandments in order. Is there any doubt in your mind that your fellow church members, who are not, like you, students of the Word preparing for the Gospel ministry, could not do any better, and that perhaps even the majority of them could not name *all* the Ten Commandments in *any* order?

D: Sadly, I have no doubt that is true.

I: But there is more. The Scriptures say of Zechariah and Elizabeth that "they were both righteous before God, walking blamelessly in all the commandments and statutes of the Lord."[5] This couple, favored as parents of John the Baptist, was described as righteous before the Lord, because they walked not only in the *commandments* of the Lord, but in His *statutes* as well.[6] Now, I wonder what those "statutes" might have been?

D: I suppose, the laws governing diet, cleanness, sacrifices and offerings, holy days, and civic responsibilities?

I: And are those statutes to be included along with the commandments in what we think of as the Law of God?

D: I believe that at least certain of them have traditionally been so regarded.

I: Undoubtedly. And can you begin to enumerate all those statutes, which Christian tradition tells us are part, together with the Ten Commandments, of the Law of God? Or can you explain which, if any, of those statutes still have validity for the followers of Christ? Or if there are any changes in the ways we should regard and interpret those statutes? Or whether they have any relevance to our living righteously

_____
[5] Luke 1.6
[6] Cf. Deuteronomy 10.12, 13

before the Lord today, as they undoubtedly did in the days of Zechariah and Elizabeth?

D: Hardly.

I: And what about your fellow church members?

D: Not a chance. I see why you might think that I may require some further persuading concerning the Law of God as ground for Christian ethics. Intellectually the idea is not alien or unwelcome. In practice, though, it's clear I need to become more familiar with and engaged in the Law of God. Which I'm not likely to do unless I am first persuaded of its utter importance for Christian faith and life. I'm beginning to be very interested in your proposition.

I: Very well then; let us proceed to examine the idea that the Law of God is the proper ground for Christian ethics.

2. The Purpose of the Law

I: I want to argue that the Law of God is the ground for Christian ethics, the soil from which a life of beauty, goodness, and truth must grow and flourish among those who have heeded the Savior's call to come and follow Him. We would do well, in making such an assertion, to begin by considering the Law of God in its original purpose. Why did God give His Law to Israel in the first place?

D: Clearly it could not have been in order that they might be redeemed.

I: You are correct, and this is a point we must establish from the beginning, and insist on over and over throughout the course of our investigation, lest we be misunderstood. Israel's redemption out of Egypt came as a gracious act of God as He moved to fulfill promises made to Israel's forebears in a previous generation.[7] Only after God had powerfully and miraculously intervened on their behalf – effecting their release from the Egyptians and their deliverance through the Red Sea – did He bring them before Him at Mt. Sinai and, through Moses, give them His Law.

D: It's clear, therefore, that we have no basis whatsoever for ever thinking that the people of God were – or are – to be saved by any form of keeping the Law of God.

I: Certainly. That is, not of their *own* keeping of the Law. However, had *Jesus* not fulfilled the righteousness of the Law, we would have no righteousness to appeal to in seeking reconciliation with the Lord. But Jesus' righteousness, made perfect through obedience, suffering, and resurrection, suffices for all who look to Him in faith.[8]

D: Yes, of course. But *we* do not keep the Law in order to be saved.

I: No, for the Law of God is never *unto* salvation, but *for the sake of it.*

---

[7] Exodus 2.23, 24
[8] Romans 3.21-26

D: "For the sake of it"? I'm not sure I understand.

I: Let me explain. Continuing His grace to Israel, whom He had redeemed, God gave them His Law in order that they might fully know, enjoy, and prosper in the deliverance He had accomplished for them. Here was a numerous people, many generations removed from anything like freedom, responsibility, or stewardship of their own land and possessions. God had rescued them from bondage, but now what? How would a people, raised as slaves, deprived of all property and liberty, their every move choreographed day by day by uncaring tyrants, how would such a people be able to move into those precious promises – which motivated God's saving act on their behalf – and be able to live in such a way as to enjoy those promises as fully as possible?

The answer is, God's Law. By receiving the Law of God and living within and according to it, Israel, a redeemed and delivered people, would enjoy the full bounty of the salvation of God and become a people holy unto the Lord.

D: But they never did.

I: Actually, never *could.*

D: Never *could?*

I: Yes. But more on that at the proper time. We are at the moment investigating the reason why God gave His Law to Israel in the first place, and I think it is clear that He gave His Law – holy and righteous and good[9] – in order that this people whom He loved might be able to enjoy the fullness of life which He had promised their fathers, and for which He had rescued them from the misery of Egypt.

The purpose of the Law – that Israel might enjoy the fullness of God's deliverance – is made clear to us by revelation subsequent to the events of Mt. Sinai, although, in retrospect, we can see the fullness of that purpose, at least by implication, in the original giving of the Law. By searching the Scriptures we may discover more of the details of God's purpose in giving the Law to Israel for the sake of salvation. That

---

[9] Romans 7.12

purpose becomes clear from six perspectives, as we consider six ways the Law of God functioned for the sake of Israel's salvation.

D: Hold on a second; let me get something to write with.

I: Go right ahead.

Ready?

D: Ready.

I: Very well. First, the Law of God functioned for ancient Israel, for the sake of their salvation, by serving to *constitute the chosen people as a nation holy to the Lord*. The Law they were given, and by which God expected them to live, was unlike anything any other nation had ever known. As Israel kept the Law, the nations around them would wonder at their uniqueness, and remark the excellence and wisdom of that body of Law that defined them as a peculiar people among the nations of their world.[10]

D: But isn't it true that the laws of other nations, contemporary with, and even prior in time to, ancient Israel reflect some elements of the Law of God?

I: The key phrase is "some elements." The fact that certain ancient law codes share similarities with that of ancient Israel is undoubtedly due to the fact that God has written the works of His Law on the hearts of all men.[11] People, merely by virtue of being people, have some knowledge of God and of His Law.[12] It was inevitable that some of that innate knowledge of God would find its way into the moral codes of the nations. But no nation had in such completeness the revealed will of God for the identity and conduct of a nation's life. Only Israel could boast that, and it was their having received the Law of God, with all its trappings and protocols, that set them off as a peculiar political entity in their day. The Law thus identified who would be the people among

---

[10] Deuteronomy 4.1-8
[11] Romans 2.14, 15
[12] Romans 1.18-20

11

whom the drama of God's salvation would be played out before the nations.

D: Does this explain why being "cut off" from the people was such a drastic act of punishment?[13]

I: Precisely, nearly as drastic as the death penalty. Put yourself above the Law of God, and you put yourself outside the people for the sake of whose well-being that Law was given. It also explains why, when Israel as a nation rejected the Law of God, they were removed from the very land that had, by that time, come to bear their name. Because, by virtue of their persistent disobedience, they were *not* Israel, they had no right to occupy the land that had come to bear that name because it had been promised to the people bearing that name.

D: To be Israel, the people of God, was to be the people known for their obedience to the Law.

I: Yes, indeed – and *now* as well as then, as we shall see.[14] Shall I continue?

D: Please.

I: Very well. The Law of God functioned for the sake of Israel's salvation by being the principal means of God's constituting His delivered people as a unique nation before the nations of the earth. A second perspective on this purpose may be seen in how the Law of God served to *indicate the way of life*.[15] Remember, Israel had been a slave people for generations. They did what they were told, lived where they were assigned, worked as they were commanded, and had no freedom to decide on such things as buying and selling, relating to neighbors, ordering a community, and so forth. What did they know about being a nation? Nothing. How were they to *learn* about such matters? God Himself showed them in His Law. Not that the Law addressed every specific situation that might arise as the people began to make a nation together. But the Ten Commandments and the statutes that go with

---

[13] Cf. Leviticus 20.1-6
[14] Cf. 1 John 2.1-6
[15] Leviticus 18.1-5

them could mark out trajectories to guide people in how to think about new and unfamiliar situations, and how to bring their daily lives into as much of the path of life as had been clearly revealed through Moses.

D: Like Constitutional law and case law in American jurisprudence?

I: Yes, rather like that. The more the Law was read, taught, learned, and put into practice, the more it would come to mold the mindset and practice of the people, and to characterize the social and cultural consensus of their communities. And the more they and their communities would know the favor of the Lord, as He had promised.[16]

Related to this is a third perspective on the Law by which it served to allow Israel to enjoy the fullness of her deliverance. The Law of God *defined the nature of sin*. It showed Israel where the way of life lay, and it warned her of the signposts leading to the path of death. Frequently, during the giving of the Law to Moses, God compared His Law with the ways of the surrounding pagan peoples. *That* way, Israel was to understand – the way of the pagans – was *not* the way of life, but of rebellion and death. No matter how attractive that way might have seemed, or who may have been wooing them to consider that path, there was to be no mistaking the fact that, according to the Law of God, the way of the pagan nations was the way of disobedience, disapproval, judgment, and death.

D: My friend seems to have fallen into the trap of mere self-interest that is the rallying cry of so many of our unbelieving contemporaries. I can see that, had he embraced the Law of God as the ground for his ethic, he would have been able to see that the ways of unbelievers are not the ways Christians are to live.

I: I feel quite certain that your friend understood that very well, at least at the intellectual level. But *knowing* the way of God's blessing and being able *to walk* in that way are two entirely different things. We'll talk a little more about this later.

---

[16] Deuteronomy 28.1-14

A fourth perspective on this overarching purpose of the Law of God comes into focus: the Law served to *demarcate the realm of liberty* for this formerly slave nation.

D: The laws of the Egyptians had led to the enslavement of Israel. God instructed His people that the practices of the pagan nations around them – practices encouraged and sustained by pagan laws, whether written or unwritten – would only enslave them again, but in a new and more spiritual and deadly way.

I: You are precisely correct. The chains and bonds of the Egyptians became metaphors for the chains and bonds of idolatry and pagan immorality. That way led to a kind of bondage that kept one from enjoying the fullness of life as God intended it for those He had come to deliver. If His delivered people would escape those bonds and live in true freedom, they must receive and embrace the Law of God, and let it guide all their conduct in their relationships with God and men.

D: Conversely, if they would *not,* they set themselves apart from the Law of God, and, by implication, from the people of Israel, and were, consequently, cut off and sent packing.

I: That was the design of God's Law, at least. Those who would not live in the freedom God provided must be recognized as the slaves to sin they had chosen to be, and identified by one and all as not part of the people of Israel. Persistence in the Law – a lifetime of obedience – was the only way of ensuring that the deliverance into which they had entered would be fully realized throughout their lives.

D: The perseverance of the saints as opposed to "once saved always saved"?

I: I suppose, if one is given to theological cliché, you could summarize it thusly.

We are considering the purpose of the Law of God as it was originally given, which was?

D: Let me see…I have it written here: to enable Israel, a people redeemed by grace, to move into and enjoy the fullness of their deliverance as a holy people unto the Lord.

I: The Law of God is not *unto* salvation…

D: …but *for the sake* of it.

I: The Law was designed to accomplish this purpose by constituting Israel as a holy nation, defining the way of life, warning against the way of sin, and leading the people into the liberty for which God had set them free from bondage to wicked, unjust laws and false deities.

A fifth perspective on this purpose shows us that the Law of God served to *awaken in God's people their constant need of His renewing grace.* Israel's inability to keep the Law – we said we would speak more of this, and we shall – meant they would always be falling into sin and be in danger of defining themselves as no longer the people of God. In His grace, God constituted His Law so that means were available within it to repair any breech that might arise between God and His people, as well as among the people themselves. Holy days, sacrifices and offerings, protocols for cleansing and sanctifying – all these provisions stood in the Law and beckoned hapless sinners to reach out through God's means to attain God's grace and be renewed as God's people. In order for Israel to enjoy full and abundant life with God, in the covenant of promise made to their forebears, they would need *constant* grace, *continuous* grace, and the Law of God provided the *way* to that grace through the avenue of priest and sacrifice. A Hebrew, convicted of sin, oppressed by his transgression, and fearful of falling under the disfavor of God, could hurry to his priest and enter into a prescribed sacrifice, and through these *legal* means be renewed in the grace of God, and recover the path of full and abundant life with Him.

D: Only an Israelite who treasured his status as one redeemed by God – who loved the God Who had redeemed him – would be so scrupulous in such matters.

I: Yes, and each time he came to the priest, offering in hand, he would not be seeking to *attain* salvation, but to *renew* salvation. He would be doing a work – a work of confession and contrition, leading to a change in his behavior – but he would not have understood that work as *achieving* salvation, but as *renewing* a salvation freely bestowed by the same God Who graciously provided these means of renewal, and gratefully received and pursued by the one who thus understood the purpose of the Law. And each such act of penitence, faithfully entered into for the sake of renewal, would affirm to penitent, priest, and public alike that here was one who valued the redemption of the Lord, loved the God he had offended, and diligently sought to enjoy more of Him and of the life for which he had been redeemed.

D: What could be clearer than that?

I: A final perspective on the purpose of the Law is the culminating facet, the one that brings all the others together into one glorious gem of grace. As Israel lived within the framework of the Law of God they would both *know and express the power of the Law unto love of God and neighbor.*[17]

God is love, as the Apostle reminds us.[18] To know God is to know love. To bear the image of God is to express His love in time. The Law of God both encodes the love God has for His people and guides them in knowing that love and expressing it to Him and to their neighbors.

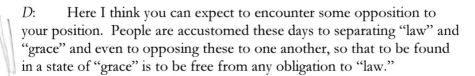

D: Here I think you can expect to encounter some opposition to your position. People are accustomed these days to separating "law" and "grace" and even to opposing these to one another, so that to be found in a state of "grace" is to be free from any obligation to "law."

I: I am well aware of this view, and we shall examine it in due course. For now, does not our Lord Jesus affirm that all the Law and all the prophets – who may be regarded as exponents of the Law – find their fulfillment in love for God and neighbors?

D: Who can deny it?

---

[17] Deuteronomy 6.4, 5; Leviticus 19.18; Matthew 22.34-40
[18] 1 John 4.8

I: Then the connection between the Law of God and the life of love is firm and unbreakable. For God's people to know the full joy of their redemption – deliverance from bondage and misery into the freedom of life and love for God and neighbors – they would have to follow the path marked out by the Law of God. The Law of God was given for the sake of salvation by leading Israel into a life of love.

Can you see now why I say that the Law of God was given *for the sake of* salvation, and not *unto* it?

D: I can, yes: Israel, a people saved by grace, would need to be instructed in the way of life for which they had been redeemed, a life of holiness before the Lord, a life of great and precious promises inherited from their forebears. So God gave them His Law, so that they might learn the ways of salvation in and through it. The Law would make them a holy people. It would bring them into fullness of life. It would warn them against sin and returning to misery and bondage, and, at the same time, guide them into liberty from lies and deception. The Law would teach them how to depend on the grace of God, and would guide them to be a community characterized by love for God and neighbors. In all these ways the Law of God functioned for the sake of Israel's salvation, to help them enjoy the fullness of the new life for which they had been delivered out of the misery of bondage in Egypt.

I: Nicely summarized. Shall we continue?

3.   The Primacy of the Law

I: The Law was God's second greatest gift to Israel.

D: The first being their redemption?

I: Precisely. Having *been* redeemed, a gift of undeserved grace, based on promises to Israel's fathers, the people of Israel would have to learn what *use* to make of that redemption, in order to enjoy it as fully as possible. The Law of God was given in order to provide that instruction. It follows – does it not? – that God intended His Law to have primacy of place among His people, at least, when it comes to their religious and ethical conduct.

D: That seems clear.

I: Yes, but let us not take the proposition for granted. For there are six ways we can discern the high place, the primacy of place, God attaches to His holy, righteous, and good Law. And, as we shall see, that primacy of place for the Law of God remains unchanged throughout the Scriptures.

D: Excuse me, but is it not enough to say that, because the Law of God was intended for such a high and holy purpose – to lead the redeemed of the Lord into the full enjoyment of their salvation – it should have primacy of place in all their affairs?

I: It would seem so, but sinful and skeptical as we are, God is not content to leave matters to mere common sense. He reinforces the primacy of His Law for His people by six indications.

First, God indicates the primacy of His Law by establishing it as a kind of *hermeneutical key* for His people, a guide to interpreting all His subsequent revelation to them. Now I must qualify this aspect of the Law at once, for, as our Lord Jesus pointed out, He Himself is *the* hermeneutical key of all Scripture.[19] All the Old Testament looks forward to Christ, demonstrates the need for Him, creates an anticipation of His coming, provides specific details concerning His Person and work, and points the

---

[19] John 5.39

readers forward to the day when, through His Anointed One, God would accomplish everything revealed in His promises and Law.[20] And all the New Testament derives from the impetus and achievement of Christ, pointing backwards and forwards to Him at one and the same time.

So, in the larger scope of Scripture, Jesus is the one true hermeneutical key Who unlocks all the meaning of God's holy Word. The Law of God, however, functions in a similar way – as a guide to interpreting all the rest of Scripture – as even Jesus Himself seems to have known.

D: Can you give me an example?

I: I shall give you several. First, notice that all the revelation of the Bible leading up to the giving of the Law serves, in one respect, to help Israel understand her identity and mission – the culmination of which, as we have seen, is in her being constituted as the redeemed people of the Lord and being called and privileged to live in His salvation according to His Law. Thus all of Genesis and the first part of Exodus leads up to those climactic chapters of God's first revelation, Exodus 20 through the end of Deuteronomy, in which He gave them His Law, the corpus of revelation designed to help them understand why they are who they are, and what it means for them to have been where they've been, as well as where they were going.

Second, note that God specifically declared that His Law was to be the standard for conduct of the people of God, including, we may assume, their conduct in teaching and preaching: "Cursed be anyone who does not confirm the words of this law by doing them."[21] The Law of God was given as the touchstone for all of life – every relationship, role, responsibility, vocation, and situation. In later generations false prophets were exposed on the ground of their having departed from the plain teaching of the Law of God. God's Word in the Law was the key by which all prophetic claims were to be tested.

Third, Jesus Himself referred to the Law in clearing up a difference of interpretation between Himself and the Tempter. When, during the temptation in the wilderness, Satan sought to wrest certain of the psalms

---

[20] 2 Corinthians 1.20; Matthew 5.17-20
[21] Deuteronomy 27.26

to his own advantage, Jesus dismissed his interpretation by referring the psalmist's meaning to the prior and primary revelation of God in the Law. Satan invited Christ to test God's promise of angels to sustain Him; Jesus said the Law says not to put God to the test.[22] In so doing He was proving His stature and calling as the great Prophet of God, promised to Israel as Moses' successor, yet squarely based on Moses as His primary hermeneutical referent.[23]

D: Please, can you give me the short version?

I: OK, let's try this: Anywhere you may be reading in the Bible, correct understanding of the text will, in some measure, be dependent on knowing the Law of God. In a larger and more complete sense, every place you may be reading will point you to Jesus. But for the interpretation of a text in its immediate setting, and for understanding its application to our own situations, knowledge of the Law of God is indispensable. This centrality of the Law of God in understanding all His revelation indicates the high place God intends the Law to have among His people.

D: Thank you.

I: The second way that God indicates the primacy of His Law is by establishing it as the *standard of love* – a role which we have previously mentioned as the culminating facet of the purpose of the Law. All the Law – and all the prophets as well, the primary interpreters of the Law in the Old Testament – is summarized in the great commands to love God and one's neighbor.[24] God Himself is love, the Apostle John advises,[25] and then proceeds to instruct us, not surprisingly, that to keep the commandments of the God of love Who gave them is, in fact, to fulfill the requirements of love.[26] Made in the image of God, people are made for love. It is their highest calling and greatest achievement. But it is only so because, by loving, which they do as they keep the commandments, they display the very character of God to the world and

---

[22] Matthew 4.5-7
[23] Deuteronomy 18.15-19
[24] Matthew 22.34-40
[25] 1 John 4.8
[26] 1 John 5.1-3; 2 John 6

21

inject something of His holy, righteous, and good purpose into human affairs.

D: It seems quite clear from the Apostle John that "to love" and "to keep the commandments" are interchangeable ideas.

I: I don't see how it can be seen otherwise.

D: I come back then, to the question of why so many Christian teachers today want to oppose grace to Law, rather smugly – it seems to me – insisting that they are "under grace" and "not under Law"?

I: This stems, I believe, from a fundamental misunderstanding of the nature and purpose of the Law, as well as of its use. If you can be patient, I think we shall come to this problem in due course.

D: Sure. Sorry.

I: Not at all. God is love; God's intention for human beings is that they should live in love – for Him and for one another. God's standard for love is His Law, and the fact of this indicates that, in God's mind, the Law is of highest primacy of place in the divine economy.

Along these same lines, in the third place, the Scriptures teach us that understanding the Law of God is also the *key to wisdom*. Even the simplest person can know a measure of divine wisdom – that "skill in living" that leads to blessedness and prosperity and is so lavishly illustrated in Solomon's Proverbs – by attending to the teaching of the Law of God.[27] Conversely, no one can claim to be wise who rejects the Law of God, as the Lord through Jeremiah indicates.[28]

And does this not make perfect sense? James instructs any who seek wisdom to seek it from God, and to expect to receive a wisdom which looks remarkably like the embodiment of love, its motive and fount.[29] Now God would have us to be wise, as Paul advises,[30] and, in order for us to be wise we must give heed to the will of God revealed in His Word, beginning in His Law. The Law had primacy of place in Israel, and it

---

[27] Psalm 19.7
[28] Jeremiah 8.8, 9
[29] James 1.5, 3.17
[30] Ephesians 5.15-17

continues to have it today, because of its salutary ability to engender wisdom in those who attend carefully to it.

D: I think of Paul saying that "all the treasures of wisdom and knowledge" are hidden in Christ.[31]

I: Yes?

D: Well, since Jesus came to fulfill all the Law, and since in Him are hidden all the treasures of wisdom, this would seem to confirm what the Scriptures elsewhere say about the Law as the key to wisdom. Jesus was supremely wise and perfectly obedient to the Law. If *we* would be wise – and, thus, be like Jesus – we also, it would seem, must apply ourselves to the Law of God as of the highest primacy in attaining the wisdom from God.

I: I could not have said it better. There is a fourth indication of the primacy of place God intends His Law to have among His people. Do you agree that the people of God in every generation are called to be holy?

D: Certainly. It is the testimony of Scripture in all its parts.

I: For instance?

D: Well, let me think. I know it occurs in the Law, but I don't know exactly where right off the top of my head.

I: How about Leviticus 11.44 and 45?

D: Let me see…yes, there it is. And Jesus quotes from this, or at least alludes to it, in the sermon on the mount, in Matthew 5, I believe.[32]

I: Right again. Anywhere else?

---

[31] Colossians 2.3
[32] Matthew 5.48

D: Yes: Paul exhorts us to work at "bringing holiness to completion in the fear of God"[33] and Peter teaches that we have been constituted a "holy nation" in Christ.[34]

I: Just as Israel, delivered out of slavery, had been constituted a holy people, a people separated unto God, by the giving of the Law at Mt. Sinai?

D: I hadn't thought of that before, but yes.

I: And does it make sense that the followers of Christ, redeemed to be a holy nation, called to pursue holiness and to be holy as God is holy, should have as their *standard* of holiness something other than what Israel was provided and Paul described as the holy and righteous and good Law of God?[35]

D: Not at all.

I: So then, in pursuing holiness, in order that we might be holy and fulfill our calling as a holy nation, we can take no other standard for holiness than the Law of God?

D: Undoubtedly so.

I: Which indicates once more…

D: …the primacy of place God intends His Law to have among His people.

I: There is a fifth indication of the primacy of the Law, one that is consistently overlooked by commentators and teachers. How do you respond to the statement that the work of keeping the Law of God is a primary work of the Holy Spirit of God?

D: I'm not sure I've ever given that idea much thought.

---

[33] 2 Corinthians 7.1
[34] 1 Peter 2.9
[35] Romans 7.12

I: All right, but how do you respond to it? Can you see, based on what we have said thus far, why this *must* be so?

D: Do you mean by virtue of the fact that He is, after all the *Holy* Spirit?

I: Exactly. Is it reasonable to expect that the *Holy* Spirit would have as a primary agenda the outworking of that holiness in the people to whom He has been sent, to dwell with them, and to be in them?[36] Or, to put the matter more directly: the Holy Spirit is God come to dwell with and in those who have been redeemed. He is the power at work within us, to will and do of God's good pleasure, exceeding abundantly above all that we could ever ask or think.[37] Does it not make sense to think that the working of His power should be toward the end of conforming us to the holiness of God – Father, Son, and Spirit?

D: It makes perfect sense, of course.

I: But you haven't given this much thought before?

D: Well, no. I tend to think of the Holy Spirit in terms of the *fruit* of the Spirit...

I: The first portion of which is?

D: Love.

I: The standard for which is?

D: Huh...the Law of God!

I: And you also perhaps think of the Spirit in terms of His role in giving gifts for the edification of the Body – the building of the community, the *nation*, of God's people?[38]

D: Yes, that would be next.

---

[36] John 14.15-17
[37] Philippians 2.12, 13; Ephesians 3.20
[38] 1 Corinthians 12.7-11

25

I: And, as we have seen, what has God given His people as the primary source for establishing them as a holy nation before Him?

D: His Law, of course. So the outworking of the fruit and gifts of the Spirit will take the form of the fulfilling of God's Law in the lives of His people?

I: It could not be otherwise, at least, if God's Word through Ezekiel is true. Read these words for me, right here, verses 26 and 27.

D: "And I will give you a new heart, and a new spirit I will put within you. And I will remove the heart of stone from your flesh and give you a heart of flesh. And I will put my Spirit within you, and cause you to walk in my statutes and be careful to obey my rules."[39] Wow!

I: By which we conclude that bringing the Law of God to fulfillment in the lives of His people is a primary work of the Holy Spirit, poured out into the Church, by means of which, as He does this, the love of God is shed abroad in our hearts.[40] And this is yet another way that God indicates the primacy of place His Law must have among His people.

D: It could not be otherwise.

I: One more indication of the primacy of the Law remains, and that is the Apostle John's declaration that obedience to the Law of God is the mark of true discipleship. It will be well to quote him here, I think: "And by this we know that we have come to know him, if we keep his commandments. Whoever says, 'I know him,' but does not keep his commandments is a liar, and the truth is not in him, but whoever keeps his word, in him truly the love of God is perfected. By this we may be sure that we are in him: whoever says he abides in him ought to walk in the same way in which he walked." That's 1 John 2, verses 3 through 6.

D: My friend's confession of faith, even his work in the pastoral ministry, apart from obedience to the Law of God, is all in vain?

---

[39] Ezekiel 36.26, 27
[40] Romans 5.5

I: We should be careful about concluding this. Your friend has had a serious lapse of obedience, which indicates he has not embraced the Law of God as the ground for his personal ethical behavior. But we must leave room for repentance, for, if he truly knows the Lord, he will not long be able so easily to live with this compromise, this act of open rebellion against the goodness of God, but will, like the prodigal son, soon enough find his way back to his senses again. And then it will be well if there are those who love him ready to embrace and take him in, and to set him on a course of rehabilitation and renewal in the Lord.

D: To quote Billy Crystal, "It'll take a miracle."

I: Perhaps, but, happily, miracles are not beyond the capacity of our God.

4.   The Promise of the Law

I: I might say just a few more words about the primacy of the Law before we turn to look at its promise. Throughout Scripture we can see many ancillary indications of the primacy of place God intends His Law to have in the lives of His people. He commands them to have the Law of God on their hearts – that is, to desire it, long for it, love and delight in it, and so forth.[41]

Further, He tells us that the person who is pleasing to the Lord, and delights in His Law, devotes his or her mind to the contemplation of the Law continually.[42] He counsels us over and over to seek understanding of the Law so that we might gain the full benefit of it.[43]

So high a place was the Law of God to have in the life of ancient Israel that her king was expected to produce a copy of the Law in his own hand, to have it read and approved by the priests, and to keep it with him wherever he went and to meditate in it daily.[44]

Even the Apostle Paul, that great exponent of grace, after arguing that all attempts to gain a righteousness unto salvation through obedience to the Law are doomed to failure, nevertheless asserted the abiding establishment of the Law of God as our standard of holiness, righteousness, and goodness in Christian conduct.[45]

And the Apostle James, that most eminently practical of New Testament writers, advises us that we should conduct our lives like people who expect to be judged by God's perfect Law of liberty.[46]

D: In the face of so much evidence regarding the primacy of God's Law, how is it that well-meaning, Christ-loving people have come to place such little stock in the Law? Why don't we know the Commandments, or care about the statutes and precepts of the Law, and

---

[41] Deuteronomy 6.6
[42] Psalm 1.2
[43] Cf. Psalm 119.12, 18, 34, 130, etc.
[44] Deuteronomy 17.18-20
[45] Romans 3.19-31, 7.12
[46] James 2.12

why do we so easily allow other presuppositions and priorities to be the determining factors...

I: The ground.

D: ...yes, the ground – for our ethical conduct as Christians?

I: These are excellent questions; we might suggest many answers for them, but I fear this would take us a little far afield from our proposition, which is that the Law of God is the ground for Christian ethics.

D: I'd still like to discuss it sometime.

I: Sometime, perhaps. For now, may I move on to yet one more topic that emphasizes the soundness of taking the Law of God as the ground for Christian ethics?

D: By all means.

I: We have said that the Law was given as an act of God's grace, to help Israel live free of the misery of sin as a holy, loving people before the Lord. Herein lies a *promise* attending to the Law of God, a promise rooted in God's covenant which we may examine in more detail.

However, it might be thought by some that Law and promise are incompatible concepts. If you have promise, then, well, a promise is a promise, whether or not I fulfill my end of the deal. And if Law is the bottom line, then nothing is promised, everything is earned. Paul anticipated this kind of confusion and asserted emphatically that the Law, which came many years after the promise made to Abraham, did not cancel out that promise.[47] Instead, it became for Israel – or, I should say, *might* have become for Israel – the means to realizing the promise.

Again, imagine Israel gathered around Mt. Sinai in the desert – a slave people, suddenly free by the hand of a God Whose power could only be described as staggering. He had called them out to be His people, to realize the promise made to their forebears, a memory of which they must have retained, be it ever so faint. "How, Lord," they must have

---

[47] Galatians 3.17

asked, "how shall we lay hold on that promise and thus realize our calling as Your people?" "Keep my Commandments," came the consistent reply.

D: But Israel did not.

I: Again, *could* not. Israel *could* not keep the Law, for their hearts were burdened with sin – as are the hearts of all men – sin so deep-seated and persistent that the offerings of beasts and other sacrifices could not remove it, but only cover it for a season. Those sacrifices had to be repeated again and again because the people of Israel *could not help their disobedience*, since they had no heart for God.[48]

D: But this did not excuse their disobedience. The prophets wailed on them about that.

I: No, of course not. It did not excuse their disobedience, for, as we have mentioned, those who were truly contrite would repair to the Law for grace in order to know cleansing, forgiveness, and renewal; however, for the most part, the people chose merely to go through the motions of religious faithfulness without any real heart of love for the Lord.[49]

D: But, in the Gospels – I think it's Luke – aren't there what amount to "Old Testament saints" who were actually looking forward to the promise of redemption and renewal?[50]

I: Yes, and people like Simeon give us a glimpse at what genuine Old Testament believers were like. They lamented the sinful plight of their nation and themselves, and their inability to escape the power and consequences of their sin, and they looked longingly toward the day they recognized all the Law and prophets were foretelling, when God would come finally to redeem them and enable them to keep His Law, know His promises, and be His people at last. The *promise* of the Law – all the blessedness it held out to an obedient people – was strictly dependent upon God accomplishing a further, final act of redemption, by which *He*

---

[48] Deuteronomy 5.29; Hebrews 10.1-4
[49] Cf. Psalm 50.7-18; Isaiah 1.12-20
[50] Luke 2.25

would put the Law on the hearts of His people[51] and *He* would give them the power to obey unto blessedness.[52] Thus Zechariah, John the Baptist's father, when he understood the meaning of John's birth, sang praise to God Who, in the coming of the Messiah, would fulfill the promise made to Abraham *and* enable the people of God to "serve him without fear, in holiness and righteousness before him all our days."[53] Zechariah's excitement was because the promise would now be fulfilled by God's coming among His people, so that they *could* and *would* obey Him unto blessedness, unto the realization of six compelling promises held out in God's covenant and realized through obedience to the Law.

D: Did you say, "six"?

I: That's right, there are six compelling promises, first articulated to Abraham, which are realized through obedience to the Law for all those who, redeemed from slavery to sin by the suffering and resurrection of Jesus, and indwelled by the Spirit of God, now earnestly long for those promises, enough to obey God's Law as the mark of true discipleship.

D: You seem to have a thing about the number six – six facets of a purpose, six indications of primacy, and now six promises.

I: It seems to be taking some hold in your attention.

D: OK, OK – six promises of the covenant, realized through the Law.

D: Remembering, of course, that, in the first instance, *the* obedience to God's Law that brings us into the promises of God is the obedience of Christ, as we have said. *Our* obedience, enabled by the Holy Spirit, is only made possible by Christ's obedience, and is always incomplete and imperfect. So that we can never claim that *our* obedience *entitles* us to anything. *Christ's* obedience is the basis of our justification *and* our sanctification. Our obedience is only made acceptable to God *through* Christ and *in* His Spirit. It is – or must be – *real* obedience, nonetheless; however, we take no credit for it, and give thanks and praise to God

---

[51] Jeremiah 31.31-34
[52] Ezekiel 36.26, 27
[53] Luke 1.68-75

alone, Who, in all our obedience, is at work within us to will and do according to His good pleasure.[54]

All right then: first, obedience to the Law brings the promise of *blessedness*, or *shalom*.[55] Shalom is that state of well-being that God created people to enjoy in the beginning. It is a combination of peace, safety, security, happiness, prosperity, and goodness that reflects the communion existing in the Godhead itself between the Persons of the Deity. This is what Jesus prayed for His disciples – and us[56] – in His great High Priest's prayer of John 17, which we can expect to realize as we are sanctified by the Word of God.[57] Shalom is the state of rest, reconciliation, restoration, and renewal that exists between people and God, His creation, and one another as a result of the obedience of faith. For those redeemed through the obedience, suffering, and resurrection of Jesus, obedience to the Law, in the strength of the Holy Spirit, brings the promise of blessedness, or, shalom.

D: So everyone who desires to know real peace must come to Jesus, and through Jesus, to the Law – living as He did – to recall John.[58]

I: Yes. There are no shortcuts. Peace with God, peace with the world, and peace with other people – which is what blessedness entails – is through the obedience *of* Christ and obedience *to* Christ, that is, to His Law.

Now a second promise is equally desirable: Obedience to the Law brings the promise of *distinction* – a "great name," as God put it to Abram.[59] The first generation to have received the Law distinguished themselves through *dis*obedience, and died in the wilderness, a forgotten and ineffectual generation. As Moses stood before the next generation and prepared to give the Law of God to them, he told them that obedience to the Law would make them the kind of people their neighbors would marvel to observe.[60] They would stand out as possessing a wondrous

---

[54] Philippians 2.12, 13
[55] Genesis 12.1, 2; Isaiah 48.18
[56] John 17.20
[57] John 17.17-26
[58] 1 John 2.3-6
[59] Genesis 12.2
[60] Deuteronomy 4.6-8

Law and serving an altogether unique God, and this would lead to their having great influence among the nations, as we shall see.

We see the power of that great name during the early years of King Solomon's reign, when he was yet walking in the wisdom of God, according to His Law, and ruling and leading the nation accordingly. Israel was veritably the center of the world at that time, with nations sending gifts and ambassadors to honor Solomon and to learn from him the ways of wisdom.[61] Israel's power to command so much notice was not, in the first instance, military, but moral. God blessed Israel in those early years of Solomon's reign – made His shalom prevail there – because of their obedience; and the nations flocked to Jerusalem from far and wide to behold the glory of Solomon's court and to share in the blessedness of this distinguished people and their king.

Now if I may just hurry on to the third and fourth promises, because they are related to this second one?

D: Certainly.

I: In the third place, God promised that Israel's distinctiveness, as she obeyed His Law, would make her an object of *attraction*, as we have seen. No nation would be able to ignore her; rather, every nation would be compelled to make some response to Israel and her distinctive morality and religion. For some the attraction would be positive, while for others it would be negative. Some nations would bless Israel, and seek closer relations. Others would curse her, and seek to do her harm. But God would intervene for her and use the nations whose notice she had attracted – whether for blessing or cursing – according to the larger purpose of His promises to His people.[62]

Then, fourth, God promised that those nations positively attracted to Israel would be *influenced* by her for good.[63] They would gain the benefit of God's common grace as they incorporated aspects of Israel's Law into their own systems. But even those nations that opposed Israel and her God would, as Israel persevered in obedience to Him, be compelled to

---

[61] 1 Kings 10
[62] Genesis 12.3; cf. Micah 4.1-5
[63] Genesis 12.3; cf. Micah 4.3

adopt some of her ways, even if out of nothing more than mere self-interest.[64] Israel's Law would affect the way the nations ordered their civil affairs. And this promise remains true for the Church. As the followers of Christ persist in obedience to His Law, He brings the benefits of His rule to the nations that host His Church. We have seen this throughout history, especially in our own country from the beginning, and continuing to this day. And there have been many nations, over the centuries, where the Name of Christ has not been warmly embraced, but the values of God's Law have had influence nonetheless. And there have been many nations which, because their historic roots were tied up with the promulgation of the Gospel, continue to show the influence of God's Law in their legal and moral codes.

D: So you're saying that those six promises made to Abraham may justly be claimed by those who believe in the Gospel?

I: Well, yes, but not on my own authority. This, after all, is Paul's point in Romans 4. All those who, like Abraham, relate to God by faith – faith which has Christ and His work as its object - instead of seeking to earn favor with God by works, share in the promises God made to Abraham, which promises Israel was urged to pursue through obedience to the Law, as are we in our day.[65] As in Abraham's day, and Moses', so in ours: "If you know these things, blessed are you if you do them."[66] "If you love me, you will keep my commandments."[67]

Let me just summarize the fifth and sixth promises. In the fifth place, God promised that, as His people walked in obedience to His ways, He would make them a *great nation*, that is, great in numbers – like the dust of the air, the sand of the seas, or the stars of the sky.[68] Israel would be fruitful and multiply, as God intended from the very beginning.[69] And then, finally, Israel would know *extension and continuance* for generations

---

[64] Cf. Psalms 66.3, 81.15, especially in the NAS ("feign obedience")
[65] Romans 4.13-16
[66] John 13.17
[67] John 14.15
[68] Genesis 12.1; Isaiah 48.19
[69] Genesis 1.26-28

upon generations to come, throughout the course of human history, and among all nations and peoples.[70]

These six promises – of blessedness, distinction, attraction, influence, greatness, and extension – are held out to those who demonstrate trust in the Lord by obedience to His Law. We cannot claim to have true and valid faith in God where no obedience to the Law is present: "Show me your faith apart from your works, and I will show you my faith by my works," as the Apostle James has it.[71] Israel in the Old Testament could not obtain these promises, because the people lacked a heart properly tuned to obedience. In the New Covenant, God works on the hearts of His people, sends His Spirit to teach and empower them, and leads them in the obedience of faith that results in their obtaining the promises, all of which find their full realization in Jesus Christ and becoming transformed into His image.[72] It is for just such good works, works of obedience to the Law, that we have been born again through faith in Jesus Christ.[73] As we, redeemed by grace, follow in the path established by the Law, trusting God and longing for his great and magnificent promises,[74] we blossom from the ground of the Law into the fruitful works of holiness, righteousness, and goodness which are the proof of our salvation.[75]

D: The promises attached to the Law would seem to provide strong incentive for embracing a Christian ethic.

I: I could not agree more.

---

[70] Genesis 12.3; Isaiah 51.8
[71] James 2.18
[72] 2 Corinthians 1.20; 3.12-18
[73] Ephesians 2.5-10
[74] 2 Peter 1.4
[75] Romans 7.12; Matthew 7.20

5.   The Practice of the Law

D: So this begs the "so what" question, doesn't it?

I: You mean the question of what we are now to *do* with the Law of God?

D: Yes. Since God had such a powerful purpose in mind in giving the Law, and since He emphasized in so many ways its primacy, and attached to obeying the Law so many wonderful promises, all those who truly know Jesus will desire to make the most of the Law for attaining the fullness of their salvation, even as He Himself did – to walk as He Himself walked, as John says.[76]

I: You put that very well.

D: Thank you.

I: And you are quite correct. "If you love me, you will keep my commandments." The question of how to *keep* the Law – the *practice* of the Law, if you will – is logically next for our consideration.

D: And you are going to tell me that there are six practices related to keeping the Law which, as we take them up, can help us to realize the purpose of the Law, establish its primacy in our own lives, and enable us to lay hold on its promises with greater efficacy.

I: You are an astute person, you know.

D: I pay attention well.

I: I shall indeed offer six aspects of an approach to the practice of the Law. But, before that, may I just refer to one episode in the ministry of Jesus that can help to bring our discussion thus far into clearer focus?

D: By all means.

---

[76] 1 John 2.6

I: You know the story of Zacchaeus.[77] See how perfectly in this story the purposes, primacy, and promise of the Law dovetail together via the mechanism of the Gospel to bring the blessing of salvation to a wretched sinner.

Here is this awful man, a tax collector. He hasn't got a friend. He knows he is a sinner, knows, that is, that his collaboration with the Romans has enabled him to cheat and steal from his neighbors with impunity and to great material advantage. But he was ill-at-ease with this situation, knowing, as he did, that the Law of God was unto holiness, and he was out of accord with that standard, and, thus, rightly to be condemned, not just by his neighbors, but by God Himself.

This wretched little man hears that Jesus is coming his way. What did He know of Jesus? Doubtless, that He was a wise and prophetic teacher. That He had done many good works, and had stood up to corrupt authorities without flinching. But, perhaps most of all, that He had shown mercy to wretched men, and offered them the hope of forgiveness and salvation. Zacchaeus had to see this man. The guilt with which he lived, because of his violation of the Law, drove him to seek out the One Who alone could grant him pardon and a new life. The Law of God drove Zacchaeus to seek the grace of God, just as God intended.

Confronted by Jesus, Zacchaeus calls Him, "Lord." He acknowledges Jesus' office and authority, and readily accedes to it – a clear and undoubted statement of faith. Then he declares his intention, according to the Law of God, to make restitution for his wickedness. Zacchaeus' first priority as a new convert is to get right with the Law. He will give his ill-gotten wealth to the poor and pay back fourfold whatever he has taken, just as the Law of God prescribes in Exodus 22.1 and elsewhere.

Now, observe Jesus' response to Zacchaeus' declaration of faith and repentance: "Ah, truly this man has come to an experience of saving grace!" His determination to obey the Law was, for Jesus, the proof that salvation had come to his house. And then, "He also is a son of Abraham," an heir, that is, of the promises of the Law. Obedience to the Law proved Zacchaeus' salvation and qualified him for admission to the promises of Abraham. Law, Gospel, faith, obedience, promises of

---

[77] Luke 19.1-10

righteousness, peace, and joy in the Spirit – all right there in this one simple story.

D: Well, clearly, it's all there.

I: Yes. So then, how do we begin to practice the Law in such a way as to prove our salvation, gain access to the promises of God, and bring to bloom from the ground of the Law an ethic of holiness, righteousness, and goodness in God's Spirit?

There are, as you surmised, six aspects of the practice of the Law of God that all must begin to master who would realize the purpose, primacy, and promise of the Law as the ground for Christian ethics.

First, the practice of God's Law is, above all, a *matter of the heart*. It must be the fervent resolve of every believer to bend his heart to learn and to perform the Law of God, and his constant prayer that the Lord God would incline his heart to these vital matters.[78]

D: The practice of the Law begins in the heart, then? In prayer?

I: Yes, but not only prayer. The heart is, so to speak, "the heart of the matter" in all aspects of the life of faith. It is the wellspring of our affections. Every desire or longing, all our hopes and aspirations, our strong passions and zeal, every sentiment of love or hate, has its origin in that part of the soul which Scripture refers to as the heart. And both the Old and New Testaments tell us that getting our hearts right and keeping them that way are the first order of business in every area of life.[79] We must be intentional and vigilant concerning the attitude of our heart toward the Law of God. The Scriptures speak much about the affections we should be nurturing toward the Law. Just looking at the psalmist, for example – here, scan with me – we can see that, in our hearts, we should

---

[78] Psalm 119.10, 32, 34, 36, 112
[79] Cf. Proverbs 4.23; Matthew 15.18, 19; Luke 21.34

be cultivating steadfastness,[80] delight,[81] longing,[82] love,[83] confidence,[84] hope,[85], resolve,[86] joy,[87] and fear[88] toward the Law of God.

D: As opposed to indifference, casualness, or even scorn, I suppose?

I: Yes, those affections show up in our hearts like weeds in a garden. They infiltrate the ground, rob the true seed of its nourishment, grow up quickly, and block the light, so that the true seed cannot come to bloom. They must be rooted out through the hard work of prayer, study, teaching, accountability, and the like, and, at the same time, and by the same means, we must train our hearts to sustain those affections which will find us ever more inclined toward learning and obeying the Law of God.

If we do not begin our practice of the Law of God by disciplining our hearts, we shall, ultimately, have no ability to stay the course of obedience for the long haul. And it is that perseverance in the commandments – issuing in love for God and neighbor – which, as we have seen, is the mark of a true follower of Jesus Christ.[89] The practice of the Law begins in the discipline of the heart. Every true believer must identify and root out those affections which keep us from the Law, and cultivate instead those which draw us to it more and more.

In the second place, the practice of the Law must *engage our minds.* The Law comprises a significant body of literature, and it cannot be learned apart from faithful reading, careful meditation, diligent study, and dutiful application. The reading and study of the Law – devoting our minds to learning it – will follow when our hearts are revved up to seek the Law. Then we can, again, following the psalmist in Psalm 119, plead with God for the understanding we need in order to be faithful in our obedience.[90]

---

[80] Psalm 119.5
[81] Psalm 119.16, 24, 35, 47, 70, 77, 92, 143
[82] Psalm 119.40, 81, 131
[83] Psalm 119.47, 48, 97, 127, 163, 167
[84] Psalm 119.66, 86, 172
[85] Psalm 119.74, 114, 147
[86] Psalm 119.106, 145
[87] Psalm 119.111, 162
[88] Psalm 119.120
[89] Revelation 14.12
[90] Cf. Psalm 119.7, 15, 27, 29, 34, 48, 59, 66, 99, 124, 148

Let's reflect a few moments on what such a regimen of learning might include. Where would you start?

D: I suppose I'd start by memorizing the Ten Commandments…in the right order.

I: An excellent idea. But how would you *use* the Commandments once you had memorized them?

D: Well, I could, let's see…I could use them during my prayers. I could meditate on them, and, as I do, listen to see if the Spirit convicts me of any sin?

I: I think that would be an excellent practice to help you in understanding and applying the Law to your own life. What else?

D: Well, didn't you say the kings of Israel were supposed to read in the Law every day?

I: I did; not actually, I, though; the Lord speaking through Moses.

D: Wouldn't that be a good thing for the people of God as well – you know, what's good for the goose is good for the gander?

I: Yes, but what would that look like? How would *you* take up such a discipline?

D: Hmmm…Read the Law once a year?

I: That would be a good start.

D: But that won't get me meditating on the Law *daily*. What if I… like, I have a friend whose wife, as part of her daily devotions, writes into her diary a verse or two from whatever she's read from that day. Then, whenever she checks her schedule, or her to-do list, there's the verse, staring right up at her. What if I did something like that with one of the Commandments or statutes of the Law each day, say, on a 3 x 5 card or something?

I: I'm sure that would be useful. Plus, you would begin to develop
a trove of cards, one or two of which you could easily take with you each
day.

You'll also want to devote yourself to some more earnest study of the
Law – wrestling with the texts, sermons or commentaries from saints of
the past, helpful books, courses at your church, and other more formal
and concentrated efforts, so that you turn the deep soil of the Law,
revealing its freshness and potency more and more. And if you can find
another person with whom you can share your learning, and learn from
him, why, that would just about be a complete discipline for devoting
your mind to learning the Law of God.

D: Do people do this? Do you know people who have such a
discipline of the Law?

I: Does that matter? It happens that I do, but that's strictly beside
the point. Each of us must engage a regimen of disciplines toward the
Law that will lead to increasing understanding of the Law for our daily
lives. It doesn't matter if *no one else* is doing this; you and I must one day
give account of our stewardship of the Law to the Lord Jesus. Let us not
be caught ashamed on that day.

A third practice is also necessary. We must make the Law of God
increasingly the formative element of our *consciences*. We must, that is,
establish and guard the primacy and priority of the Law in every aspect of
our lives. Paul indicates that the conscience – the valuing center of the
soul – interacts with the heart and the mind either to confirm or excuse
our conduct in any matter, and to lead us into the practice of love.[91] The
more the Law of God serves as the "default mode" of our consciences,
the greater is the likelihood that our hearts and minds will be properly
tuned to the Law, issuing in choices and behaviors that lead to promise
and blessing. Similarly, the more we nurture our hearts and tune our
minds to the Law, the stronger will its primacy grow in our consciences.

Again, the psalmist testifies in numerous ways to his having established
the Law as the top priority of his soul. Look at just a few references: he
declared he had made a conscious choice to learn and obey the Law, and

---

[91] Romans 2.14, 15; 1 Timothy 1.5

that he had sealed that choice with a promise and an oath.[92] He determined to hate everything which was contrary to the Law.[93] He preferred the delight, contemplation, and practice of the Law more than sweet food or vast riches.[94] Now such a priority of place in one's conscience does not come without some diligent and continuous effort. His rehearsal of these matters in writing – and subsequent reading and re-reading of them, we may assume – may well have been a way of reminding himself of the primacy of the Law in matters of conscience, of reinforcing that primacy, and of inviting his readers to hold him accountable for this as well.

By some such means we also must establish the primacy of the Law in our consciences, like a cornerstone in our souls, so that all future growth and development of our souls will follow the shape and direction laid down by the Law.

With our souls now wholly determined to the Law of God – heart, mind, and conscience – we may begin to concentrate on the actual *practice* of the Law in daily obedience. We must always keep in mind, in the fourth place, that the practice of the Law is a *matter of life*, of the choices we make and the courses of action we pursue.[95]

D: If I'm diligent in working at giving the Law primacy of place in my soul – heart, mind, and conscience, as you say – won't *obedience* to the Law just come naturally? Won't it just "be there" when I need it?

I: The only thing that comes "naturally" to us is sin. The law of sin within us is so powerful – well, consider even the Apostle Paul. Near the end of his career, after so many fruitful labors, and such faithfulness, he still described himself as the "chief of sinners."[96] He had wrestled with that law of sin from his earliest days as a believer, and he knew he would continue to do so all his life on earth.[97] He understood that he would always have to pay careful attention to the goings-on of his life,[98] that he

---

[92] Psalm 119.30, 57, 106
[93] Psalm 119.126, 163
[94] Psalm 119.72, 103
[95] James 1.22-25
[96] 1 Timothy 1.15
[97] Romans 7.7-25
[98] Ephesians 5.15-17

would never be free of the spiritual warfare that sought his undoing,[99] and that he would always have to work hard to realize the full promise of his salvation, the glorious blessedness of obedience in Jesus Christ.[100] What was true for Paul is doubtless true for us as well.

Or consider Peter, urging his readers to "give all diligence" in bringing to fruition those virtues and attributes consistent with obedience to the Law.[101] He did not exhort those believers just to work on their souls, but to practice in daily obedience the patterns of holy, righteous, and good conduct set forth for them in the Word of God, beginning in His Law.

So, while working on getting our souls in sync with the Law helps to ensure that the aptitude or inclination or tendency to obedience is present within us, we will always have to give conscious effort, in any situation, to *do* what the Law requires in leading us to show love for God and our neighbors. At the same time, we will recognize that every time we *do* succeed in obeying God's Law, it is no credit to us, but to the Spirit of God at work in us, willing and doing according to God's pleasure, and shedding the love of God abroad in us.[102]

D: So when Paul says "work out your salvation," he means we have to work at it every day.

I: That's right, every day, and every step of every day.

Now it's true, as you indicate, that the more we love the Law, the better we understand it, and the more firm our resolve to let it have the primacy in our conduct, the greater is the likelihood that we will, in fact, live out its requirements in the strength of the Spirit. But simply *knowing* what the Law says, even *delighting* in the idea of its outworking in us, will not suffice to bring us the blessedness that comes from obedience. We must put the Law into practice, in our personal lives, in our communities as believers, and in every area of culture and society where we can have influence for good.

---

[99] Ephesians 6.10-20
[100] Philippians 2.12, 13
[101] 2 Peter 1.5-11
[102] Philippians 2.12, 13; Romans 5.5

In so doing there will be a fair measure of trial and error, mutual encouragement and instruction, accountability and cooperation, and, of course, confession and repentance. But as we look to the Lord to teach and guide us, we may reasonably expect that the fruit of a true Christian ethic will begin to bloom from the ground of God's Law that we are dutifully and faithfully tilling in our souls.

And, lest you might think that working at the Law like this is an onerous burden, let me remind you of the ways the psalmist spoke of his relationship to the Law – delight, joy, zeal, love, and all the rest. Obedience to God's Law, out of a well-tuned soul, in the power of the Spirit, and unto Christ-likeness, is the greatest adventure, the most exhilarating and satisfying way of life anyone could conceive. It is righteousness, peace, and joy in the Holy Spirit, the very sum and substance of life in the Kingdom of Jesus Christ.[103]

D: I don't know many people who would agree with that statement.

I: I have no doubt. But then, you don't know many people who know or obey the Law of God, do you?

D: Well, that's true.

I: There is a fifth matter related to the practice of the Law that I'd like to develop just a bit.

D: Right. Sorry.

I: No, no, not at all. I just want to make the point that people who have never embraced the Law in the way we've been describing are "naturally" going to think that studying and obeying the Law is an onerous task, a burden, a yoke they must bear, and that it's somehow linked to legalism and salvation by works. But you can see, I think, that this is not at all what I'm saying, or what the Scriptures teach about the practice of God's Law.

D: I can now, that's for sure.

---

[103] Romans 14.17-19

I: Good. Then let us hasten on to my fifth point, which is – and I've already alluded to this earlier on in our conversation – that our practice of the Law of God must include both the practice of the Ten Commandments and of those statutes, precepts, and rules which yet have some valid application in our lives.

D: Such as?

I: Well, let's back up a bit. First, I have no doubt that you will agree that the work of Jesus Christ our great High Priest in offering Himself as the perfect sacrifice for our sins has done away with all the statutes of the Law related to sacrifices and offerings.[104]

D: Certainly.

I: Christ has done away with the old priesthood, and has established a new priesthood, both of Himself as our perpetual Intercessor[105] and of all believers as priests to God and one another.[106] Further, He has given us new statutes, precepts, and rules for carrying out our work as priests – things like the sacraments, prayer, mutual teaching and exhortation, burden-bearing, and so forth, which I don't want to unpack just now, but perhaps at another time.

So all the statutes, precepts, and rules of ancient Israel that related to the work of the priests have been set aside and replaced. That would include the laws concerning sacrifice, vestments, particular liturgical activities, and various kinds of cleansing. Now those laws still have value to us, in that they reveal something about the character of God, and they remind us of what God requires of those who would live in obedience to Him. But we no longer need to observe the *particulars* of those laws; the general principles they contain instruct us, but not toward specific acts of obedience.

Of the laws regulating Israel's diet, we may say that they are no longer valid, as the Lord twice made a point of setting those laws aside in the New Testament.[107] Again, when we understand those laws in their

---

[104] Hebrews 10.1-10
[105] Hebrews 7.25
[106] 1 Peter 2.9
[107] Mark 7.19; Acts 10.9-16

original setting, against the backdrop of pagan dietary practices, the primitive state of nutritional knowledge, and Israel's call to be distinct, we can see a certain wisdom that, in general terms, can lend us guidance even today. But the particulars of those laws we may safely ignore, as relates to our own pursuit of the blessings of God.

That leaves the civil laws of Israel: what are we to do with them?

Let me make two observations concerning the civil laws. First, it seems quite clear from the New Testament that the Lord Jesus and the Apostles held those civil laws to have some abiding validity for the practice of Christian ethics. We have already observed the situation involving the conversion of Zacchaeus. We also find the Apostle Paul, in at least two situations, demonstrating his conviction that the civil statutes of ancient Israel still have application to the followers of Christ. In his apology for reviling the high priest, contrary to the Law of God, and in his indicting the Corinthians for their failure to support his ministry, Paul turned to the civil code of Israel as his basis for action and instruction.[108]

The Apostle James also, warning against those who play fast and loose with the Law of God, cited the civil law forbidding evil speech against one's brother, and the one warning the rich not to cheat those in their employ.[109] Apparently, as James understood it, to live as those who believe they will be judged by the law of liberty[110] means to live according to the Ten Commandments and the civil statutes of Israel.

So we have solid New Testament guidance for believing that the civil laws of ancient Israel yet have something important to contribute to the soil of a Christian ethic.

At the same time – and this is my second point – we must recognize that the conditions of the Kingdom of God and the age of grace make new demands on our interpretation and use of those statutes in the practice of Christian ethics.

D: What do you mean by that?

---

[108] Acts 23.1-5, cf. Exodus 22.28; 1 Corinthians 9.1-12, cf. Deuteronomy 25.4
[109] James 4.11, 12, cf. Leviticus 19.17, 18; James 5.1-4, cf. Deuteronomy 24.14, 15
[110] James 2.12

I: I mean, we must remember that ancient Israel was a theocracy, in which society was governed under a seamless cope of religious and civil law, by priests, judges, and kings, each assigned their separate roles in the interpretation and application of those laws. The followers of Jesus Christ today do not live in such a situation. Our situation is rather more like that of Israel in exile than Israel in the land. We are called to be a peculiar people, as we have seen, but we conduct our lives in the context of a secular setting, where the "power of the sword" – the enforcing of civil statutes – is in the hands of authorities other than those who rule the believing community.[111]

Further, Israel lived in a specific historical period, in a particular social and cultural context, the conditions of which no longer obtain in our day. The change in our own social and cultural situation, together with the demands and limitations of our being a people in exile, mean that we must think rather more carefully about how to apply these civil statutes.

Already in the New Testament we see evidence of this. In 1 Corinthians 5 the Apostle Paul counseled the Corinthians how they should deal with a particularly awful situation that had arisen in their midst. A member of their church had committed fornication with his father's wife – apparently, not his own mother, and she not a member of the church. In ancient Israel this violation of the civil law was punishable by death.[112] But the elders of the church do not wield the sword. The most they could do in bringing the judgment of God against such wickedness was to separate the sinning member from the body – excommunication. And this is what Paul commands.[113] That offending brother was to be treated *as though* he were dead, and sent out into the world until the shame of his sin and heart-brokenness at being separated from the body of Christ would lead him to repentance and restoration to the church.[114]

This is but one example of our need to think carefully about how we apply the civil laws of ancient Israel to our practice of Christian ethics, but it demonstrates clearly, I believe, that the circumstances of the Kingdom – our being a nation in exile – together with the demands of grace mean that we must not allow a simple "one-to-one" application of

---

[111] Romans 13.1-6; 1 Peter 2.13-15
[112] Deuteronomy 22.30; Leviticus 20.11
[113] 1 Corinthians 5.9-13
[114] 2 Corinthians 2.5-11

those laws to be our standard for practice. Jesus taught the same, when He overruled the *lex talionis* standard of the ancient Hebrew code and signaled a need for greater grace in the practice of God's Law.[115]

This leads to my sixth point concerning the practice of the Law of God, which is that the practice of the Law of God must always be pursued within a *proper authoritative framework*. None of us may take the Law of God into our own hands and presume to be the final authority on how it is to be interpreted and applied. Christians are called to be a people under authority, and to submit to those elders duly recognized and appointed to watch over their souls for the edification of the body of Christ.[116] The interpretation of God's Law – how we are to understand and use it in pursuing a Christian ethic – must remain in the hands of the ministers of the Word and the elders who serve with them. And they, in turn, must seek the counsel of ministers and elders from every age of the Church to guide their understanding of how the Law applies to contemporary situations.

D: Wasn't that the practice in ancient Israel as well?

I: It was, indeed. In each community judges and elders were appointed, who gathered in the gates of the city to deliberate matters of civil welfare according to the Law of God in open debate, for all to see. The story of Boaz and Ruth is an excellent example of this.[117]

It was the duty of the elders of the community to lead by example and instruction with respect to the practice of God's Law. The members of the community could only gain the benefit of God's Law as they were taught and judged by it, and as they saw it lived in those who sat in the gates as God's covenant representatives. God reserved His harshest words of condemnation for those shepherds of Israel who preferred their own pleasure and convenience to the care of His people according to His Law.[118]

D: That makes me sad for my friend.

---

[115] Matthew 5.21-48
[116] Cf. Titus 1.5; 1 Thessalonians 5.12, 13; Hebrews 13.7, 17; 1 Peter 5.1-3; Acts 20.28
[117] Ruth 4; cf. Deuteronomy 16.18-20
[118] Cf. Ezekiel 34.1-11

I: And well it should. Well it should.

6.   The Perversion of the Law

I: Allow me to point out one more thing concerning the practice of the Law, which really takes up and embraces everything we said on this subject. And that is, while the Law is the *ground* for Christian ethics, it is not the *limit*. A Christian ethic, relevant to its particular time and circumstances, blossoms into beauty, goodness, and truth from the ground of the Law. But it does not realize its full potential merely in obeying the letter of the Law.

D: Again, I would be helped by an example.

I: All right then, the sixth commandment says that we must not commit murder. Do you have a problem with that commandment?

D: Not at all.

I: So you are willing, with the help of God's Spirit, to keep that commandment, thus showing love to God and your neighbor by preserving his well-being through your obedience?

D: Yes, certainly.

I: Fine. Now there are statutes related to this commandment which further help us to understand how you may promote and care for your neighbor's well-being beyond the *letter* of that commandment into the *spirit* of it, which involves the preservation and advancement of life. If you don't ever murder anyone, you will have kept the *letter* of that commandment. But you may well violate its *spirit* if you never go beyond the letter into the deeper meaning and intent of the commandment.

D: OK, but...

I: Let me finish. Now suppose you have ill feelings toward your neighbor, which you allow to fester unchecked, until a genuine hatred of your neighbor takes root in your soul. You still wouldn't think of murdering him, but you harbor hatred in your heart, a clear violation of Leviticus 19.17 and 18.

D: So when I become aware of that hatred I must confront it head-on, confess and repent of it, and begin to replace it with affections of forbearance and love?

I: Yes, that's it. But notice that the commandment does not instruct you to do so. The intent is there, clearly, but not the *specific* direction, say, to forbear with your neighbor, however insufferable and irritating he may be. You keep the *letter* of the Law by not murdering him, and by not allowing hatred to lodge in your soul. You enter into the *spirit* of the Law by nurturing forbearance and love instead. The sixth commandment and Leviticus 19.17 and 18 are the *ground* for your ethic, but the flower of it spreads the scent of forbearance and love, the commandment's true *spirit* and *intent*.

One more example: you would never murder anyone, and you're careful against hating your neighbor, even to the point of diligently stirring up affections of love for him. But the spirit of the Law requires that we go beyond even this, to actual specific deeds designed to express love for our neighbor in the form of care for his well-being. And this we do, not according to the *letter* of the Law, but its *spirit*.

D: Example?

I: You own your own home, correct?

D: I do.

I: Fine, then I assume, as it is clear you wish to be diligent in obedience to the Law, that you have built a railing around your roof, so as to protect your neighbor when he's up there?[119]

D: My neighbor's never up there.

I: But the Law expressly commands you to build a railing around your roof.

D: But we never *go* on our roof. What's the point?

---

[119] Deuteronomy 22.8

I: You never go on your roof, but does it ever snow or does ice ever form on the sidewalk in front of your home?

D: Every winter, without fail.

I: The same sidewalk used by your mailman? And probably many of your neighbors?

D: The same.

I: Do any of them ever slip on the ice and fall on the sidewalk in front of your home?

D: No, because I keep it shoveled and clear of snow and ice…Ahh, I see your point. I don't build a railing around my roof – the times and culture have changed – but I preserve my neighbor's well-being by keeping my sidewalks clear, thus showing my neighbors God's love in a simple, practical, everyday manner.

I: A manner in keeping with the *spirit* of the Law, but not its *letter.* Add a deck to the back of your house, and the building codes will require that railing for the same reason. But the statute concerning the railing implies much more concerning how we may love our neighbors as ourselves and fulfill the requirement of the sixth commandment. Only the Spirit of God can lead us into all truth in understanding how we must always show the love of God.[120] But the better we know the *letter* of the Law, and meditate on it day by day, the greater the resources of commandments and statutes the Spirit will have at His disposal to lead us in loving God and others in any particular situation.

So the *letter* of the Law is the ground for our ethic, but it cannot define the *limit.* That limit will be determined situation by situation as we – with souls and strength devoted to obedience – follow the leading of the Spirit as He engenders love and obedience within and through us, according to the Law of God.

---

[120] John 16.13

D: And then our well-tuned consciences will affirm our acts of love and confirm our testimony of faith in Jesus.[121]

I: Yes. And isn't it interesting how the Lord, in the Book of Revelation, connects our testimony of faith in Jesus with obedience to His Law?[122] Both of these are, in the final analysis, works of God's Spirit within us; but we are called to practice both of them as obedient followers of Christ. In the Spirit we profess our faith in Christ, and in the Spirit we enter into the spirit of the Law via the avenues and along the trajectories created by the commandments and statutes of God.

D: I'm sure my friend was never taught this in seminary.

I: Probably not.

D: He might have spared a great many people a great deal of pain if he had.

I: I need to say just one more thing about the Law of God.

D: And that is?

I: That we must guard against the *perversion* of God's Law.

D: Let me guess – which takes six forms?

I: No, actually – only three. But each has two aspects.

D: Of course.

I: I think I can be brief here. The first perversion of the Law of God is that which sees obedience to the Law as a *condition* of salvation – either in *obtaining* salvation or *keeping* it.

This is what most people think of when someone urges obedience to the Law of God. It is the perversion of *legalism*, a perversion of the Law that the people of God are right to abhor.

---

[121] Romans 2.15
[122] Revelation 12.17, 14.12

Some of our fellow believers will fear that, in calling for the practice of the Law of God as integral to our salvation we mean that keeping the Law of God *results* in salvation: we obey God in order to *be* saved. Others will worry that we intend to say that keeping the Law *preserves* salvation, such that, if we ever fail in obedience, salvation is lost, and must be regained through renewed obedience: we obey God in order to *stay* saved.

Either of these views of the Law is legalism, the attempt to gain or keep salvation through good works. And, of course, in arguing that the Law of God is the ground for Christian ethics, we are advocating *neither* of these views. The Scriptures squarely condemn all such efforts as doomed to fail.[123] So let us say again, plainly and emphatically, that in arguing for the Law of God as the ground for Christian ethics we do not mean to recommend any notion of salvation by works. We do not *gain* our salvation through obedience to the Law, and we do not *retain* our salvation through such obedience. Salvation is entirely by grace through faith. Those attending to our argument should have no fear whatsoever that we intend to promote any form of legalism.

However, salvation is always *unto* good works[124] such as are defined by the Law of God, and every true believer will cultivate such works as *proof* of salvation, or the logical *expression* of it, rather then as *means*.

D: It seems very difficult for most believers to grasp the distinction you make between *earning* salvation by good works and *proving* it that way. The minute you start talking about obeying the Law with most Christians I know, they immediately want to accuse you of being legalistic.

I: Well, what do they offer in place of obedience to the Law as evidence of their salvation?

D: They will talk vaguely about such things as love, the fruit of the Spirit, following Jesus…that kind of thing.

---

[123] Romans 3.19, 20
[124] Ephesians 2.8-10

I: But we have seen throughout the course of our conversation that we cannot speak meaningfully about *any* of those matters apart from obedience to the Law of God.

D: I see that now; hopefully, I'll be able to help others see that as well.

I: They are probably much closer than they realize to agreeing with you on this matter. It will take forbearance and love on your part to help them see the beauty of the Law and the power for loving that it possesses, as well as to enable them to overcome their fear that, by advocating the Law of God as the ground for Christian ethics we are recommending some form of legalism, which they are right to abhor.

May I mention the second perversion of the Law?

D: By all means.

I: The second perversion of the Law is closely related to the first. This one suggests that law is a *sufficient means* for obtaining divine favor. You are doubtless aware of Christians who teach a strict regimen of law-keeping in the belief that, if they do, God must favor their endeavors. Within the Church we find rigid moralists who insist on their rules and regulations as essential to knowing the favor of God – no smoking, no drinking or dancing, always dress just so, use this version of the Scriptures, and so forth. Failure to keep these rules and regulations may not mean that you forfeit your salvation – here is the difference from the legalism we examined previously – but you certainly must not expect God to look as favorably on you as He would if you did. Other forms of this same perversion include prescriptions to seek the Lord in specific ways for personal prosperity, or to practice certain kinds of giving in order to secure the blessings of God. Those who hold such views, in whatever form, believe they can connect all such rules and regulations, protocols and practices, to the commandments of God, such that living by their laws and guidelines is tantamount to obeying the Law of God, and is the way to find favor with Him.

Such people are often committed more to the *letter* than the *spirit* of the Law, and more to the letter as *they* interpret it than to the *Spirit* as God gives Him. They promote a kind of self-righteousness that wants to manipulate God, expecting Him to show His favor because of their strict conformity to their rules, rather than because of His grace and mercy in Jesus Christ. It can seem at times that these brethren have more love for their peculiar legal system, with its careful prescriptions of moral acceptability and spiritual success, than for either God or their neighbors.

A second form of this perversion of the Law claims that God will bestow His blessing on that nation which conforms *its* laws to *His* Law. Put another way, this view insists that the way to return the favor of God on our land is to enact laws and statutes that conform to the requirements of God's Law, and to put in office people who will sustain those laws and work for even more. Such people are not deluded into thinking that reforming our legal system means that salvation will come to all our citizens – and here is where this view differs from the kind of legalism I talked about earlier. However, they do insist that we may avert the judgment of God and expect to know His favor as a nation if we bring our laws and statutes more into line with the plain teaching of the Law of God.

D: But you don't want to suggest we shouldn't work for this, do you?

I: You mean for the laws of ours or any nation to be shaped according to the Law of God?

D: Yeah.

I: Of course I'm all for that. Certainly the Scriptures teach that the Law of God is for all people, and that even unbelievers must be held accountable to the requirements of the Law.[125] But the way to *favor* with God, *saving* favor first of all, and *ongoing* favor as a consequence, is, as we have seen, through faith in Jesus Christ. Such divine favor cannot be obtained by legal reform, but only by the awakening of God's Spirit through the preaching of the Gospel. We must not try to substitute moral, political, social, and legal reform for revival and awakening as the way to God's blessing. As we have seen, the only way to ensure long-term obedience to God – and, hence, the blessing that accompanies such

---

[125] Cf. Daniel 4.27; Matthew 14.1-4

obedience – is through the heart-change that comes with conversion to Christ and the gift of God's Spirit.

At the same time, those who have come to new life in Christ must work to reform every aspect of society and culture because it honors God to do so, and, as we have said, there is indeed blessing to be realized by such means, although not to the extent envisioned by some, and not in any kind of *sustained* way apart from awakening and revival in God's Spirit. So let us not be misunderstood as teaching that the Law of God has power in and of itself, apart from the Gospel, to ensure long-term, culture-transforming benefit, either within the Church or among the larger society.

D: Could this be seen as just another form of legalism?

I: That question might be asked, but I distinguish legalism as that perversion of the Law which relates to the *saving* favor of God, either in gaining or retaining it. The perversion I have just outlined is not so much concerned with salvation as with temporal blessings and favor. In the Church this view does not write nonconformists out of the Kingdom. It simply looks upon them as somehow less enlightened. And in society at large this view has nothing to say about salvation, only about averting temporal judgments and securing temporal blessings.

So you could call this a form of legalism, but that might confuse the matter of salvation where, in reality, salvation is not really the issue.

D: OK, I see that now. It's a fine distinction.

I: Perhaps, but an important one.

There is a third perversion which is undoubtedly the most prevalent one today. That is what is called *antinomianism*, the view that the Law of God is unnecessary for Christian faith. This perversion also takes two forms.

The first is outright denial of the need for the Law. Here we encounter those who simply reject the idea that they need to have any concern for keeping the Law of God. They have come under the grace of God, they insist, and are free from all obligation to the Law. Anyone who tries to urge obedience to the Law is simply promoting a form of legalism. These believers will look elsewhere for a ground for their ethical behavior.

D: In the light of all we have discussed, this view, for professing Christians, seems utterly impossible. How is it that so many believers today hold tenaciously to it – or so it seems to me?

I: I'm not persuaded that as many believers hold to this view as you might think. I know a good many people do rather glibly espouse a "not under law/under grace" view of their salvation, but still, consider how vocal Christians have been in recent decades over the state of the Ten Commandments in the public square. It seems that by far and away most of those who are identified with Christ continue to insist that the Law of God – well, the Ten Commandments, at least – is still valid and should still be allowed a formative role in American life. So I don't think there are that many antinomian purists, people who frankly deny any role to the Law of God whatsoever, among the followers of Christ. Among those who call themselves Christians but deny the authority of Scripture this view may be more common. Such believers tend to take their ethical cues more from the *spiritus mundi* than the Spirit of God. But among Bible-believing Christians I don't think this view has much appeal.

D: OK, but I still hear this protest all the time, and it's still the case that most believers – like my friend – have little understanding of the Law and little or no regard for it where their behavior is concerned.

I: Yes, but this is not a matter of their *denial* of the Law – the first form of antinomianism – but of their *neglect* of it, the second, and more virile form of this perversion. They simply have not developed a disciplined practice of the Law as the Scriptures teach we are to do, perhaps because there is no fear of God before their eyes.[126]

This is surely one of the great maladies in the contemporary Church, that the Law of God is neglected in the teaching and preaching of today's pastors, and that precious little of the kind of *practice* of the Law that we discussed just a little while ago is evident in the lives of God's people.

---

[126] Romans 3.18

Remember how you asked me whether I knew anyone who maintained the kind of practice of God's Law that I described?

D: Yes.

I: Your asking that question is indication of the low regard in which the Law is held in the minds of most believers. To you what I was describing as the practice of the Law was not something you had heard of or seen before. No one you know, at least, is as devoted to the Law of God as I explained is necessary for the right practice of it. It was precisely such neglect of the Law that allowed idolatry and immorality to flourish in ancient Israel, resulting in the judgment of God.[127] Why should we expect anything different when we choose to ignore the path of life, liberty, and love which God has so plainly marked out for us, the path which Jesus so diligently trod, and the path which the apostles directed us to walk if we would know true righteousness, holiness, and goodness?

D: Witness the example of my friend.

I: Go on.

D: Neglect of the Law allowed an idolatry of self-interest to take root in his soul, which led to the immoral acts of abandoning wife and ministry, and which, doubtless, will result in some kind of judgment from the Lord, if only the discipline imposed by his church.

I: Quite right. But let us not, in rightly assessing the deplorable practices of our fellow church members, put ourselves above them or fail to intercede and work for their restoration. If the Church is ever to become the joy of the whole earth,[128] the city set on a hill,[129] the moral leader of men and nations,[130] and the spotless Bride of Christ,[131] it will only be as we heed the ancient cry of the prophets of old, "To the Law, and to the Testimonies!"[132] And we shall not hear such a longing from

---

[127] Cf. Habakkuk 1.1-4
[128] Psalm 48.1, 2
[129] Matthew 5.13-16
[130] Micah 4.1-5
[131] Ephesians 5.25-27; 1 John 3.2, 3; 2 Peter 3.11; Revelation 21.9
[132] Isaiah 8.16-20

the people of God until those who lead them – and those who aspire to lead them – make the practice of the Law of the highest priority in their walk with the Lord. For only thus shall we be able to prepare a fertile ground for the flourishing of an ethic of beauty, goodness, and truth.

As Moses said in Deuteronomy 32.46 and 47, "Take to heart all the words by which I am warning you today, that you may command them to your children, that they may be careful to do all the words of this law. For it is no empty word for you, but your very life..."

So you are right to be concerned for your friend, for whose repentance and recovery we must now seek the Lord together; but let us not fail to pray for ourselves as well, that the fertile ground of the Law of God may be properly cultivated, nurtured, and developed in our own souls, and bring forth the fruit of divine love in the form of obedience to the Law of God.

The Fellowship of Ailbe

The Fellowship of Ailbe is a spiritual fellowship in the Celtic tradition. We are dedicated to advancing the rule of Christ in and through churches by working for spiritual enrichment, renewing of vision, and more effective ministry among church leaders. The Fellowship offers a variety of services, including, mentoring, training materials, seminars and retreats, and other resources available on its website, www.myparuchia.com.

T. M. Moore is Principal of The Fellowship of Ailbe. The author or editor of nearly 20 books, T. M. has over 30 years of ministry experience in a wide variety of fields. His essays, articles, reviews, and poems have appeared in national and international journals, and he continues to write for a variety of publications and websites. His weekly column, *Second Sight*, appears on the BreakPoint.org website. T. M. also serves as Dean of the Centurions Program of the Wilberforce Forum. He and his wife and editor, Susie, live at the Ailbe Center, which serves as their home and retreat center for The Fellowship in Hamilton, Va. They have four adult children and ten grandchildren.

CPSIA information can be obtained at www.ICGtesting.com
Printed in the USA
LVOW12s2340150316

479264LV00001B/112/P